D1621949

782.42
H

Headington,
Christopher
Sweet sleep

FLESH PUBLIC LIBRARY
PIQUA, OHIO

DISCARD

JAN 1993

SWEET SLEEP

Sweet Sleep

A COLLECTION OF LULLABIES, POEMS AND CRADLE SONGS

CHRISTOPHER HEADINGTON

FLESH PUBLIC LIBRARY
PIQUA, OHIO

DISCARD

Clarkson N. Potter, Inc./Publishers
201 East 50th Street
New York, New York 10022

Published by Clarkson N. Potter, Inc., distributed by Crown Publishers, Inc.,
201 East 50th Street, New York, New York 10022

CLARKSON N. POTTER, POTTER and colophon are trademarks of
Clarkson N. Potter, Inc.

Conceived and produced by Breslich & Foss, London
Anthology, typesetting and design copyright © 1989 Breslich & Foss

All rights reserved. No part of this book may be reproduced or transmitted in any form
or by any means, electronic or mechanical, including photocopying, recording, or by
any information storage and retrieval system, without permission in writing from
the publisher.

Printed in Belgium
Designed by Nigel Partridge
Musical Notation by Malcolm Lipkin

Library of Congress Cataloging-in-Publication Data
Sweet Sleep
     Summary: A collection of familiar lullabies to be sung, which includes such
familiar titles as "Rock-a-bye Baby" as well as lesser known melodies from around the
world.
                1. Lullabies, English.   2. Children's songs.
               [1. Lullabies.   2. Songs]   I. Headington, Christopher.
               M1997.S9288   1990   88-26898
               ISBN 0-517-57321-0
               10 9 8 7 6 5 4 3 2 1
               First Edition

CONTENTS

All color pictures are courtesy of The Bridgeman Art Library except
those on the following pages:
pp. 8, 22, 31, 33 and 82 (Mary Evans Picture Library)
pp. 37, 75, 84 and 87 (Fine Art Photographic Library)
p.16 (Victoria & Albert Museum)

'The Dream Shell' on p.33 appears by kind permission of
Blackie & Son Limited

'Sleep, Baby, Sleep' by Le Mair on p. 57 appears by kind permission of
Soefi Stichting Inayat Fundatie Sirdar 1990

Every effort has been made to obtain permission from copyright holders.
The editor apologizes for any omissions which may have occurred.

INTRODUCTION

Lullaby is one of the gentlest words in the English language, and the words of a lullaby are intended to have a soothing quality which induces sleep. Sounds similar to 'lull' occur in many languages and all have associations with peace and calm, from the classical Greek word used to describe waves lapping on a seashore to the several variations – lulla, lulle, lullen – found in cradle songs from European and Scandinavian countries. But the meaning is unimportant because the baby understands only the mood of the words; their 'music', in fact. The repetition of sounds, whether single syllables or whole words, often contributes to the charm of a lullaby. Lullabies are occasionally used as a warning or lament on behalf of a vulnerable child, but by far the most common sentiment is the expression of tenderness and fond protectiveness universally extended to tiny children.

This book is intended to introduce the timeless quality of traditional lullabies to new generations of parents and children. Familiar and well-loved words and melodies are here, as well as some attractive cradle songs less well known to English-speaking readers. Each tune is presented in its original form as an unaccompanied melody, progressing at moderate speed and pitched within the range of a normal voice, whether high or low. The collection will reacquaint many readers with the rich pleasures to be found in simple lullabies, which it is hoped will be enjoyed above all for their original purpose, that of sending little children into the sweetest and most peaceful of slumbers.

CHRISTOPHER HEADINGTON
JUNE, 1989

BRAHMS' LULLABY

The German composer Johannes Brahms wrote this melody (c.1868) for the first child of Bertha Porubszky, an amateur singer in the ladies' choir that he conducted.

Lullaby and good night
In the sky stars are bright.
Round your head flowers gay
Scent your slumber till day.

Close your eyes now and rest,
May these hours be blest,
Go to sleep now and rest,
May these hours be blest.

Lul-la-by and good night In the sky stars are bright. Round your head ___ flo-wers gay ___ Scent your slum-ber till day. Close your eyes now and rest, May these hours ___ be blest, Go to sleep now and rest, May these hours ___ be blest.

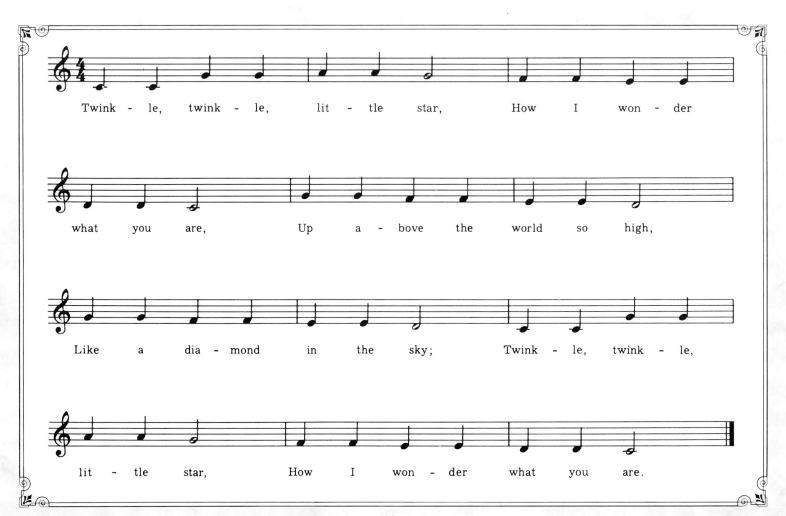

TWINKLE, TWINKLE, LITTLE STAR

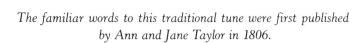

*The familiar words to this traditional tune were first published
by Ann and Jane Taylor in 1806.*

Twinkle, twinkle, little star,
How I wonder what you are,
Up above the world so high,
Like a diamond in the sky;

(Chorus)
Twinkle, twinkle, little star,
How I wonder what you are.

When the blazing sun is gone,
When he nothing shines upon,
Then you show your little light,
Twinkle, twinkle all the night.
(Repeat chorus)

Then the traveller in the dark
Thanks you for your tiny spark.
Could he see which way to go
If you did not twinkle so?
(Repeat chorus)

In the dark blue sky you keep,
And often through my curtains peep,
For you never shut your eye
Till the sun is in the sky.
(Repeat chorus)

*According to Italian tradition, a butterfly passing by the
cradle is the baby's soul.*

A CRADLE SONG

Sleep! sleep! beauty bright,
Dreaming o'er the joys of night;
Sleep! sleep! in thy sleep
Little sorrows sit and weep.

Sweet babe, in thy face
Soft desires I can trace,
Secret joys and secret smiles,
Little pretty infant wiles.

As thy softest limbs I feel,
Smiles as of the morning steal
O'er thy cheek, and o'er thy breast
Where thy little heart does rest.

O! the cunning wiles that creep
In thy little heart asleep.
When thy little heart does wake
Then the dreadful lightnings break.

From thy cheek and from thy eye,
O'er the youthful harvest nigh.
Infant wiles and infant smiles
Heaven and Earth of peace beguiles.

(William Blake)

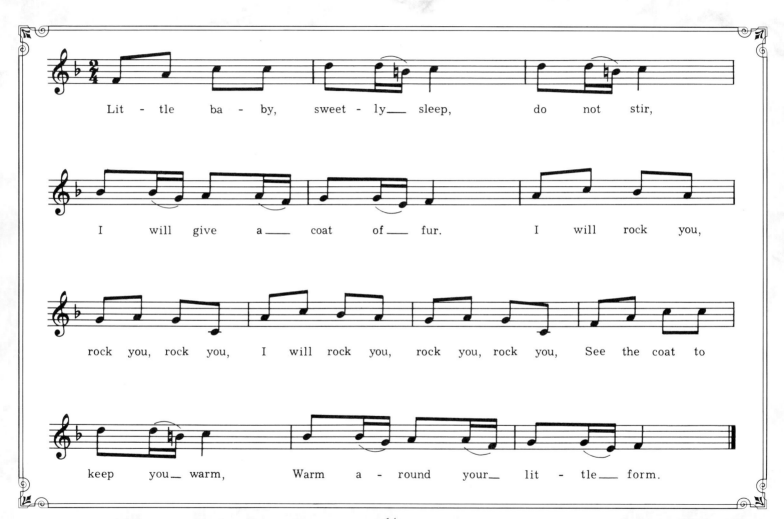

Lit - tle ba - by, sweet - ly____ sleep, do not stir,

I will give a____ coat of____ fur. I will rock you,

rock you, rock you, I will rock you, rock you, rock you, See the coat to

keep you__ warm, Warm a - round your__ lit - tle__ form.

THE ROCKING SONG

Trad. Czechoslovakian

This was originally The Rocking Carol, *addressed to the infant Jesus.*

Little baby, sweetly sleep, do not stir,
I will give a coat of fur.
I will rock you, rock you, rock you,
I will rock you, rock you, rock you,
See the coat to keep you warm,
Warm around your little form.

ALL THE WORLD IS SLEEPING
Trad. Welsh

Go to sleep upon my breast,
All the world is sleeping,
Till the morning's light you'll rest,
Mother watch is keeping.

Birds and beasts have closed their eyes,
All the world is sleeping,
In the morn the sun will rise,
Mother watch is keeping.

Go to sleep u-pon my breast,_ All the world is slee - ping.

Till the mor-ning's light you'll rest,___ Mo - ther watch is kee - ping.

Birds and beasts have closed their eyes, _ All the world is slee - ping.

In the morn the sun will rise,_ Mo - ther watch is kee - ping.

EVENING

Hush, hush, little baby,
The sun's in the west;
The lamb in the meadow
Has laid down to rest.

The bough rocks the bird now,
The flower rocks the bee,
The wave rocks the lily,
The wind rocks the tree;

And I rock the baby
So softly to sleep —
It must not awaken
Till daisy-buds peep.

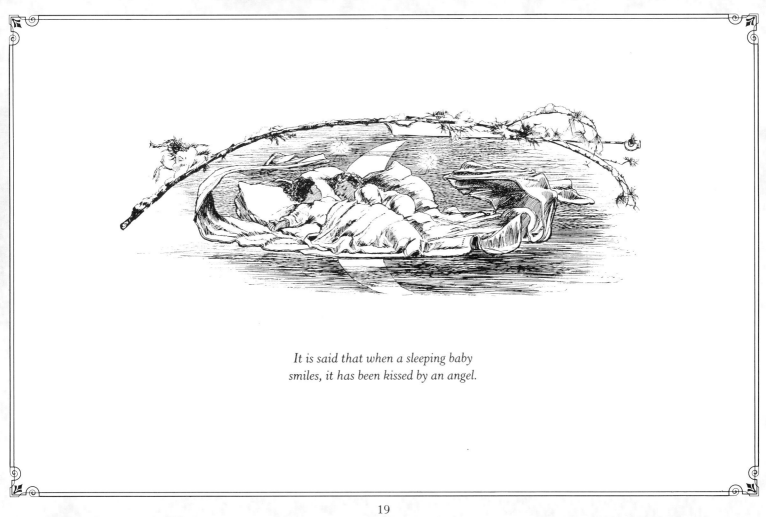

It is said that when a sleeping baby smiles, it has been kissed by an angel.

Oh dear, what can the mat-ter be? Dear, dear, what can the mat-ter be? Oh dear,

what can the mat-ter be? John-ny's so long at the fair._____ He pro-mised he'd buy me a

fair - ing should please me, And then for a kiss, Oh! he vowed he would tease me, He

pro-mised he'd buy me a bunch of blue rib-bons To tie up my bon-ny brown hair.

WHAT CAN THE MATTER BE?

Trad. English

(*Chorus*)
Oh dear, what can the matter be?
Dear, dear, what can the matter be?
Oh dear, what can the matter be?
Johnny's so long at the fair.

He promised he'd buy me a fairing should please me,
And then for a kiss, Oh! he vowed he would tease me,
He promised he'd buy me a bunch of blue ribbons
To tie up my bonny brown hair.
(*Repeat chorus*)

He promised to buy me a pair of sleeve buttons,
A pair of new garters that cost him but tuppence,
He promised to buy me a bunch of blue ribbons
To tie up my bonny brown hair.
(*Repeat chorus*)

He promised he'd buy me a basket of posies,
A garland of lilies, a garland of roses,
A little straw hat to set off the blue ribbons
That tie up my bonny brown hair.
(*Repeat chorus*)

GOOD NIGHT TO MY BABE
Trad. German

Good night to my babe and sweet be your sleep,
May silence enfold you, your slumber be deep.
Good night, good night, good night, good night.

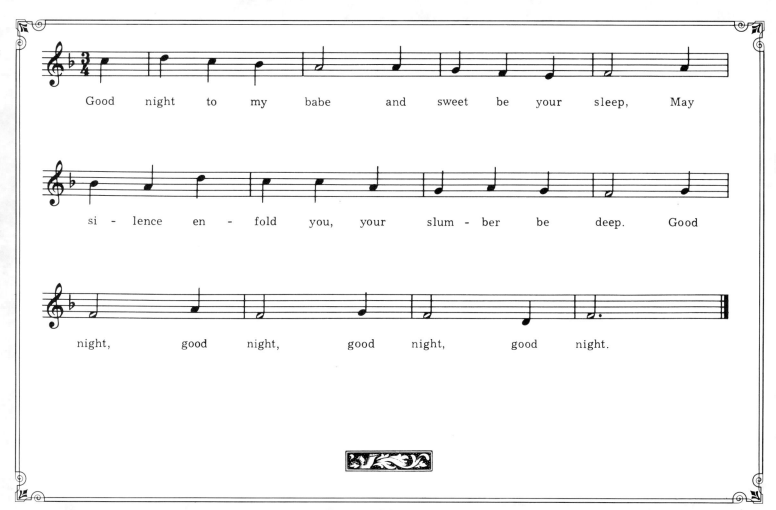

Good night to my babe and sweet be your sleep, May

si - lence en - fold you, your slum - ber be deep. Good

night, good night, good night, good night.

A BABY-SERMON

The lightning and thunder
They go and they come;
But the stars and the stillness
Are always at home.

TEDDY BEAR

Teddy Bear, Teddy Bear, turn around.
Teddy Bear, Teddy Bear, touch the ground.
Teddy Bear, Teddy Bear, show your shoe,
Teddy Bear, Teddy Bear, that will do.

Teddy Bear, Teddy Bear, go upstairs,
Teddy Bear, Teddy Bear, say your prayers,
Teddy Bear, Teddy Bear, turn out the light,
Teddy Bear, Teddy Bear, say good night.

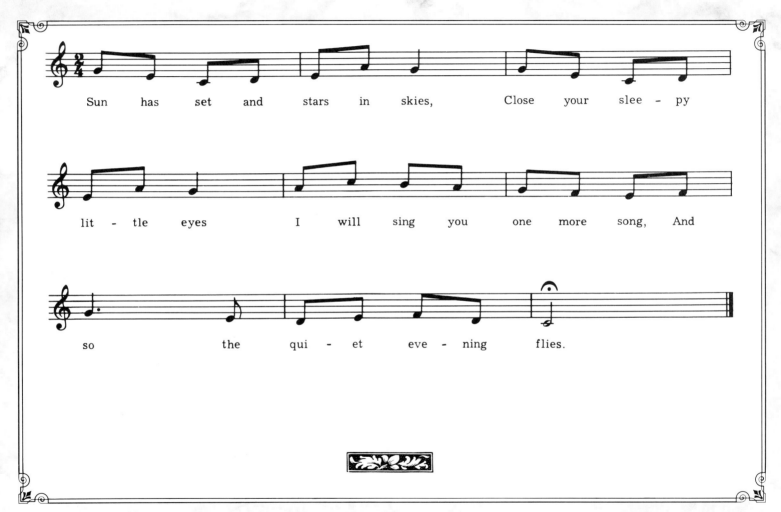

Sun has set and stars in skies, Close your slee - py

lit - tle eyes I will sing you one more song, And

so the qui - et eve - ning flies.

SUN IS DOWN
Trad. French

Sun has set and stars in skies,
Close your sleepy little eyes.
I will sing you one more song,
And so the quiet evening flies.

Star light, star bright,
First star I see tonight,
I wish I may, I wish I might,
Have the wish I wish tonight.

I see the moon,
And the moon sees me;
God bless the moon,
And God bless me.

Sleep, baby, sleep.
Thy father guards the sheep;
Thy mother shakes the dreamland tree,
Down falls a little dream for thee;
Sleep, baby, sleep.

LIE A-BED

Lie a-bed
Sleepy-head,
Shut up eyes, bo-peep.

Till day break
Never wake
Baby, sleep.

BYE, BABY BUNTING
Trad. English

*'To bunt' means to push with the head, or butt, so that a
nursing mother might use the word to describe her baby.*

Bye, baby bunting,
Daddy's gone a-hunting,
To catch a little rabbit-skin,
To put the baby bunting in,
Bye, baby bunting.

Bye, ba - by bun - ting, Dad - dy's gone a - hun - ting, to

catch a lit - tle rab - bit skin, to put the ba - by bun - ting in.

Bye, ba - by bun - ting, Dad - dy's gone a - hun - ting.

etc.

WHERE DID YOU COME FROM, BABY DEAR?

Where did you come from, baby dear?
Out of the everywhere into here.

Where did you get your eyes so blue?
Out of the sky as I came through.

What makes the light in them sparkle and spin?
Some of the starry spikes left in.

Where did you get that little tear?
I found it waiting when I got here.

What makes your forehead so smooth and high?
A soft hand stroked it as I went by.

What makes your cheek like a warm white rose?
I saw something better than anyone knows.

Whence that three-cornered smile of bliss?
Three angels gave me at once a kiss.

Where did you get this pearly ear?
God spoke, and it came out to hear.

Where did you get those arms and hands?
Love made itself into hooks and bands.

Feet, whence did you come, darling things?
From the same box as the cherubs' wings.

How did they all just come to be you?
God thought about me, and so I grew.

But how did you come to us, you dear?
God thought about you, and so I am here.

George MacDonald

LOVE ME

Love me, — I love you,
Love me, my baby;
Sing it high, sing it low,
Sing it as may be.

Mother's arms under you,
Her eyes above you.
Sing it high, sing it low,
Love me, — I love you.

Christina Rossetti

Win - kum, win - kum, shut__ your eye Sweet my ba - by,

lull - a - by. For the dews are fal - ling soft,

Lights are flick - 'ring up a - loft. And the moon - light's

peep - ing o - ver Yon - der hill - top__ capped with clo - ver.

WINKUM, WINKUM

Trad. English

Winkum, winkum, shut your eye
Sweet my baby, lullaby.
For the dews are falling soft,
Lights are flickering up aloft;
And the moonlight's peeping over
Yonder hilltop capped with clover.

Chickens long have gone to rest,
Birds lie snug within their nest.
And my birdie soon will be
Sleeping like a chickadee.
For with only half a try
Winkum, winkum shuts her eye.

BILLY BOY

Trad. English

O where have you been, Billy Boy, Billy Boy,
O, where have you been, charming Billy?
I have been to seek a wife,
She's the darling of my life,
But she's a young thing and cannot leave her mother.

Did she ask you to come in, Billy Boy, Billy Boy,
Did she ask you to come in, charming Billy?
Yes, she asked me to come in,
There's a dimple on her chin,
But she's a young thing and cannot leave her mother.

Did she have you take a chair, Billy Boy, Billy Boy,
Did she have you take a chair, charming Billy?
Yes, she had me take a chair,
She's got ringlets in her hair,
But she's a young thing and cannot leave her mother.

Can she bake a cherry pie, Billy Boy, Billy Boy,
Can she bake a cherry pie, charming Billy?
She can bake a cherry pie,
In the twinkling of an eye,
But she's a young thing and cannot leave her mother.

Did you leave her in tears, Billy Boy, Billy Boy,
Did you leave her in tears, charming Billy?
Yes, I left her in tears,
But I'll be back in a couple of years,
But she's a young thing and cannot leave her mother.

O, _____ where have you been, Bil - ly Boy, Bil - ly

Boy, O, _____ where have you been, char - ming Bil - ly? _____

_____ I have been to seek a wife, She's the dar - ling of my

life, But she's a young thing and can - not leave her mo - ther. _____

NOW THE DAY IS OVER

Now the day is over,
Night is drawing nigh,
Shadows of the evening,
Steal across the sky.

Now the darkess gathers,
Stars begin to peep,
Birds and beasts and flowers,
Soon will be asleep.

Sabine Baring-Gould

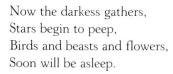

Hush, thee, my babby,
Lie still with thy daddy,
Thy mammy has gone to the mill,
To grind thee some wheat
To make thee some meat,
Oh, my dear babby, lie still.

Dance to your dad - dy, my___ lit - tle lad - die, Dance to your dad - dy,

my___ lit - tle lamb. You shall have a fish - y on a lit - tle dish - y,

You shall have a fish - y when the boat comes in. Dance to your dad - dy,

my lit - tle lad - die, Dance to your dad - dy, my___ lit - tle lamb.

DANCE TO YOUR DADDY

Trad. British (northern)

Dance to your daddy, my little laddie,
Dance to your daddy, my little lamb.
You shall have a fishy on a little dishy,
You shall have a fishy when the boat comes in.
Dance to your daddy, my little laddie,
Dance to your daddy, my little lamb.

O CAN YE SEW CUSHIONS

Trad. Scottish

*The soothing sounds traditional to lullabies are called upon here
to bring calm 'when the bairn greets' (when the baby cries).*

O can ye sew cushions and can ye sew sheets?
And can ye sing ba-loo-loo when the bairn greets?
And hee and ba, birdie, and hee and ba, lamb,
And hee and ba, birdie, my bonnie wee lamb.

I've placed my cradle on yon holly top,
And aye as the wind blew my cradle did rock,
And hush-a-ba baby, O ba-lilly-loo,
And hee and ba, birdie, ma bonnie wee doo.

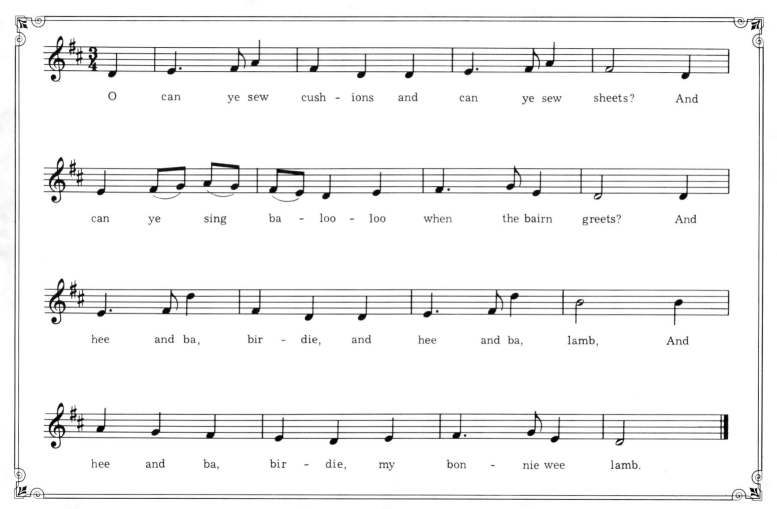

O can ye sew cush - ions and can ye sew sheets? And

can ye sing ba - loo - loo when the bairn greets? And

hee and ba, bir - die, and hee and ba, lamb, And

hee and ba, bir - die, my bon - nie wee lamb.

There is an English saying 'If you rock a cradle empty, then you shall have babies plenty.' In Scotland, however, rocking an empty cradle is thought to bring bad luck upon the family.

A BABY'S BOAT

Baby's boat's a silver moon
Sailing in the sky,
Sailing o'er a sea of sleep
While the stars float by.

Sail, baby, sail
Out upon that sea;
Only don't forget to sail
Back again to me.

Baby's fishing for a dream,
Fishing far and near,
Her line a silver mooonbeam is,
Her bait a silver star.

Sail, baby, sail
Out upon that sea;
Only don't forget to sail
Back again to me.

Au clair de la lu — ne, Mon a - mi Pier - rot,

Prê — te - moi ta plu — me Pour é - crire un mot.

Ma chan - delle est mor — te, Je n'ai plus de feu;

Ou - vre - moi ta por — te, Pour l'a - mour de Dieu.

Au Clair de la Lune

Trad. French

Au clair de la lune,
Mon ami Pierrot,
Prête moi ta plume
Pour écrire un mot.
Ma chandelle est morte,
Je n'ai plus de feu;
Ouvre moi ta porte,
Pour l'amour de Dieu.

Au clair de la lune,
Pierrot répondit:
Je n'ai pas de plume,
Je suis dans mon lit.
Va chez la voisine,
Je crois qu'elle y est,
Car dans sa cuisine,
On bat le briquet.

O HUSH THEE, MY BABY

This is from Sir Walter Scott's poem Lullaby of an Infant Chief, *addressed to a child destined to become a Scottish Highland chieftain.*

O hush thee, my baby, thy sire was a knight,
Thy mother a lady both lovely and bright:
The woods and the glens from the towers which we see,
They all are belonging, dear baby, to thee.

O hush thee, my ba — by, thy sire was a knight, Thy

mo — ther a la — dy both love — ly and bright: The

woods and the glens from the towers which we see, They

all are be — long — ing, dear ba — by, to thee.

CRADLE SONG

What does the little birdie say
In her nest at peep of day?
Let me fly, says little birdie,
Mother, let me fly away.
Birdie, rest a little longer,
Till the little wings are stronger;
So she rests a little longer,
Then she flies away.

What does little baby say,
In her bed at peep of day?
Baby says, like little birdie,
Let me rise and fly away.
Baby, sleep a little longer,
Till the little limbs are stronger;
If she sleeps a little longer,
Baby too shall fly away.

Lord Tennyson

Down with the lambs,
Up with the lark,
Run to bed children
Before it gets dark.

HUSHABYE BABY ON THE TREE-TOP

Trad. English

This famous lullaby has several variants, including Rockabye Baby. *The words were first printed in 1765, and there are at least two different tunes.*

Hushabye baby on the tree-top,
When the wind blows the cradle will rock.
When the bough breaks the cradle will fall;
Down will come baby, cradle and all.

Hush - a-bye ba - by on the tree - top, When the wind blows the cra - dle will rock. When the bough breaks, the cra - dle will fall, Down will come ba - by, cra - dle and all.

ROCK-A-BYE BABY ON THE TREE TOP

Rock-a-bye, baby, on the tree top,
When the wind blows, the cradle will rock,
When the bough breaks, the cradle with fall,
And down will come baby, cradle and all.

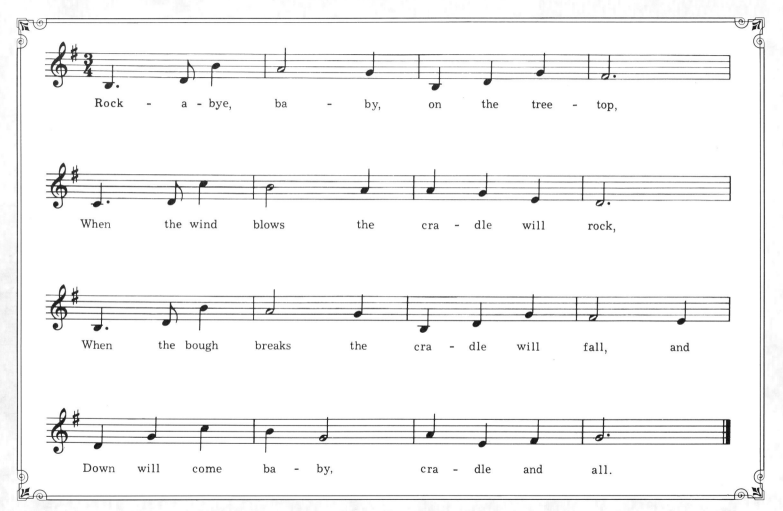

Rock - a - bye, ba - by, on the tree - top,

When the wind blows the cra - dle will rock,

When the bough breaks the cra - dle will fall, and

Down will come ba - by, cra - dle and all.

53

THE SANDMAN

This is the seventh in a series of Children's Folk Songs (Volks-Kinderlieder) *which Brahms published in 1858.*

The flowers are sleeping
Beneath the moon's soft light,
With heads close together
They dream through the night.
And leafy trees rock to and fro
And whisper low —
Sleep, sleep, lullaby,
O sleep, my darling child.

Now birds that sang sweetly,
To greet the morning sun,
In little nests are sleeping
Now twilight has begun.
The cricket chirps its sleepy song,
Its dreamy song —
Sleep, sleep, lullaby.
O sleep, my darling child.

The Sandman comes on tiptoe
And through the window peeps,
To see if little children
Are in their beds asleep.
And when a little child he finds
Casts sand in his eyes —
Sleep, sleep, lullaby,
O sleep, my darling child.

The flo - wers are slee - ping Be - neath the moon's soft

light, With heads___ close to - ge - ther They dream___ through the

night. And___ lea - fy trees rock to and fro And___ whis - per___

low — Sleep, sleep, lul - la - by, O sleep, my dar - ling child.

Rock-a-bye, baby,
Thy cradle is green,
Father's a nobleman,
Mother's a queen;
And Betty's a lady,
And wears a gold ring;
And Johnny's a drummer,
And drums for the king.

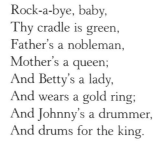

LULLY, LULLAY, THOU LITTLE TINY CHILD

This simple lullaby is taken from the sixteenth-century Coventry Carol. *It has its origin far in time, place and mood from the evening peace of the nursery, for the carol refers to the 'slaughter of the innocents' ordered by King Herod of Judaea at the time of Christ's birth.*

> Lully, lullay, thou little tiny child,
> By, by, lully, lullay,
> Lully, lullay, thou little tiny child,
> By, by, lully, lullay.

FRÈRE JACQUES
Trad. French

Frère Jacques, Frère Jacques,
Dormez vous? dormez vous?
Sonnez les matines, sonnez les matines,
Din din don, din din don.

Frè - re Jac - ques, Frè - re Jac - ques, Dor - mez - vous? dor - mez - vous?

Son-nez les mat - i - nes, son-nez les mat - i - nes, Din din don, din din don.

BABY, BYE

Baby bye, here's a fly,
Let us watch him, you and I,
How he crawls upon the walls,
Yet he never falls...
If you and I had six such legs,
We could surely walk on eggs.
There he goes, upon his toes,
Tickling, tickling baby's nose.

Lullaby, my pretty baby,
Close thine eyes so bright:
While the moon pours o'er thy cradle
All her silvery light.

*Some people believe that it is unlucky for
two women to rock a cradle together.*

SHOHEEN, SHOLYOH
Trad. Irish

This comes from County Kerry in Eire (Southern Ireland), a green and unspoiled region that lies on the south-west coast of the country. Macushla and m'leanabh (pronounced m'lanov) are Irish Gaelic words of affection. All the other Gaelic words are pronounced as spelt.

Shoheen, sholyoh, the soft shades are creeping,
Shoheen, my heart's love, the angels are near.
Shoheen, sholyoh, my darling is sleeping,
Marie's macushla, while mother is near.

Hush, O my treasure is dreaming,
Lu la, sleep on till day.
Lu la, smiles now are beaming,
Shoho, sorrows away.

Shoheen, shalyoo, in your white cradle lying,
God give you, m'leanabh, your night's sweet repose.

Sho - heen, sho - lyoh, the soft shades are cree - ping, Sho -

- heen, my heart's love, the an - gels are near. Sho - heen, sho -

- lyoh, my dar - ling is slee - ping, Ma - rie's ma - cush - la, while

mo - ther is near. Hush, O, my trea - sure is

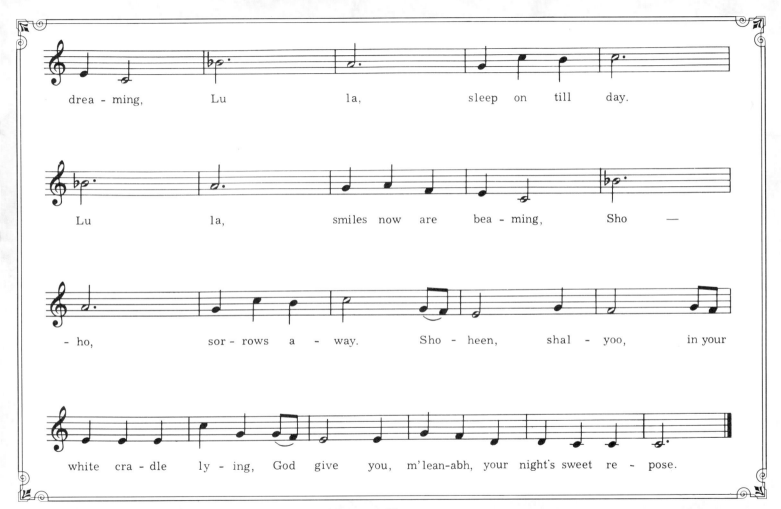

ALOUETTE
Trad. French

(Repeat full verse each time, incorporating the new words)

Alouette, gentille Alouette,
Alouette, je te plumerai.

Je te plumerai la tête,
Je te plumerai la tête,
Et la tête, et la tête.
Alouette, Alouette,
O, Alouette, gentille Alouette,
Alouette, je te plumerai.

Je te plumerai le bec,
Je te plumerai le bec,
Et le bec, et le bec,
Et la tête, et la tête,
Alouette, Alouette,
O, Alouette, gentille Alouette,
Alouette, je te plumerai.

Je te plumerai le dos.

Je te plumerai les jambes

Matthew, Mark, Luke, and John,
Bless the bed that I lie on.
Four corners to my bed,
Four angels round my head;
One to watch and one to pray
And two to bear my soul away.

THE LAND OF NOD

From breakfast on through all the day
At home among my friends I stay,
But every night I go abroad
Afar into the land of Nod.

All by myself I have to go,
With none to tell me what to do —
All alone beside the streams
And up the mountainside of dreams.

The strangest things are there for me,
Both things to eat and things to see,
And many frightening sights abroad
Till morning in the land of Nod.

Try as I like to find the way,
I never can get back by day,
Nor can remember plain and clear
The curious music that I hear.

Robert Louis Stevenson

Sweet and low, sweet and low, Wind of the wes - tern sea, _____

Low, low, breathe and blow, Wind of the wes - tern sea, _____

O - ver the rol - ling wa - ters go, Come from the dy - ing moon and blow,

Blow him a-gain to me, _____ While my lit - tle one, while my pret - ty one, sleeps.

Sweet and Low

These beautiful words by the English poet Alfred, Lord Tennyson (1809-92, appointed poet laureate by Queen Victoria in 1850) were set to music by Joseph Barnby (1838-96).

Sweet and low, sweet and low,
Wind of the western sea,
Low, low, breathe and blow,
Wind of the western sea,
Over the rolling waters go,
Come from the dying moon and blow,
Blow him again to me,
While my little one, while my pretty one, sleeps.

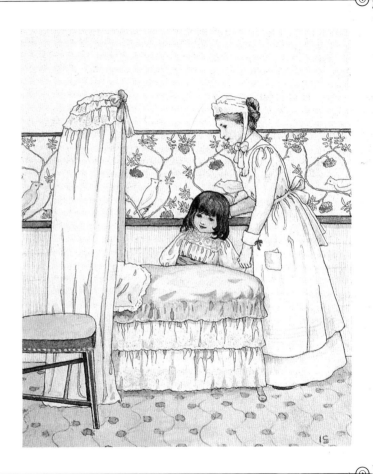

MOCKING-BIRD

Trad. USA (Tennessee)

Hush, little baby, don't say a word,
Momma's gonna buy you a mocking-bird.
If that mocking-bird don't sing,
Momma's gonna buy you a diamond ring.

If that diamond ring turns to brass,
Momma's gonna buy you a looking-glass.
If that looking-glass gets broke,
Momma's gonna buy you a billy goat.

If that billy-goat don't pull,
Momma's gonna buy you a cart and bull.
If that cart and bull turn over,
Momma's gonna buy you a dog called Rover.

If that dog called Rover won't bark,
Momma's gonna buy you a horse and cart.
If that horse and cart fall down,
You'll be the sweetest little one in town.

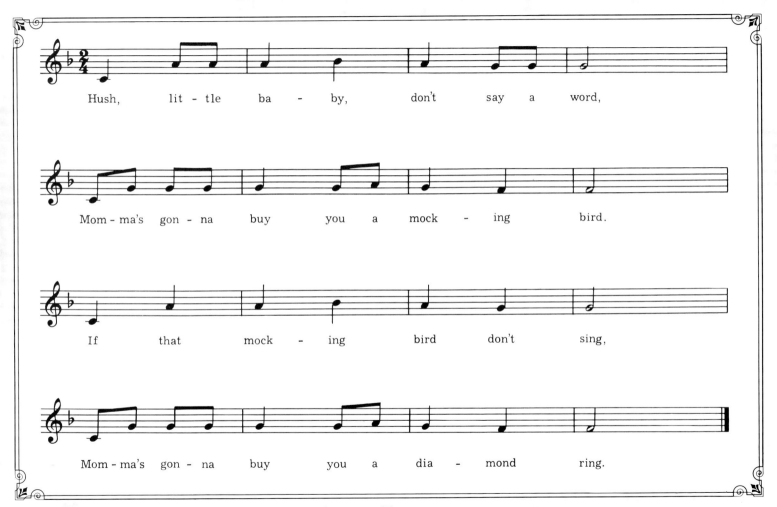

 ## CREOLE LULLABY

Dreamland opens here
Sweep the dream path clear!
Listen, chile, dear little chile
To the song of the crocodile...

ALL THROUGH THE NIGHT

Trad. Welsh

This familiar song derives from a Welsh evening hymn. The English words set to the traditional melody during the nineteenth century, a prayer for safekeeping through the night, are slightly changed in the lullaby to express the parent's care for the sleeping child.

Sleep, my child, and peace attend thee
All through the night.
Guardian angels God will send thee
All through the night.

Soft and drowsy hours are creeping,
Hill and dale in slumber sleeping,
I my loving vigil keeping
All through the night.

Sleep, my child, and peace at-tend thee All through the night.

Guar - dian an - gels God will send thee All through the night.

Soft and drow - sy hours are cree - ping, Hill and dale in slum - ber slee-ping,

I my lo - ving vi - gil kee - ping All through the night.

Sleep, lit - tle child, go to sleep, Mo - ther is here by your bed. _____

Sleep, lit - tle child, go to sleep, Rest on the pil - low your head. __ The world is si - lent and

still, The moon shines bright on the hill, _____ And creeps past your win - dow

sill. Sleep, lit - tle child, go to sleep, Go to sleep, go to sleep.

SLEEP, LITTLE CHILD

*The lilting melody of this lullaby comes from a traditional tune,
used by Mozart among other composers.*

Sleep, little child, go to sleep,
Mother is here by your bed.
Sleep, little child, go to sleep,
Rest on the pillow your head.

The world is silent and still,
The moon shines bright on the hill,
And creeps past your window-sill.

Sleep, little child, go to sleep,
Go to sleep, go to sleep.

LITTLE ONE, MY BABY
Trad. Spanish

Little one, my baby, little one, my heart!
Little one, my joy, and little one, my love!
Sleep now! sleep now!
Little one, my child, who won't go to sleep,
Time to go to sleep, time to go to sleep.
Sleep now! sleep now!

Lit-tle one, my ba - by, lit-tle one, my heart! Lit-tle one, my joy, and lit-tle one, my love!

Sleep now! sleep now! Lit-tle one, my child, who__ won't go to sleep,

Time to go to sleep, time to go to sleep. Sleep now! sleep now!

La - ven - der's blue, dil - ly, dil - ly, La - ven - der's green,

When I am king, dil - ly, dil - ly, You shall be queen.

LAVENDER'S BLUE
Trad. English

This pretty nursery rhyme is also sung as a lullaby because of its softly repetitive refrain.

Lavender's blue, dilly, dilly,
Lavender's green,
When I am king, dilly, dilly,
You shall be queen.

Call up your men, dilly, dilly,
Set them to work,
Some to the plough, dilly, dilly,
Some to the cart.

Some to make hay, dilly, dilly,
Some to cut corn,
While you and I, dilly, dilly,
Keep out of harm.

GOLDEN SLUMBERS
Trad. English

The words of this well-loved lullaby are attributed to the English
dramatist Thomas Dekker (c. 1572-1632).

Golden slumbers kiss your eyes,
Smiles await you when you rise.
Sleep, pretty baby, do not cry
And I will sing a lullaby.

Care you know not, therefore sleep,
While I o'er you watch do keep.
Sleep, pretty baby, do not cry
And I will sing a lullaby.

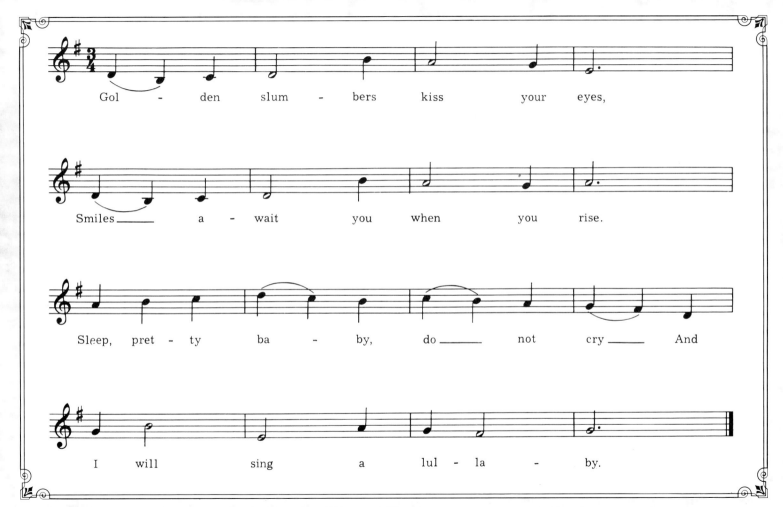

THE BABY'S DANCE

Dance, little baby, dance up high,
Never mind baby, mother is by;
Crow and caper, caper and crow,
There little baby, there you go:
Up to the ceiling, down to the ground,
Backwards and forwards, round and round.
Then dance, little baby, and mother shall sing,
With the merry gay coral, ding, ding, a-ding, ding.

Ann Taylor

SLEEPY SONG

Ere the moon begins to rise
Or a star to shine,
All the bluebells close their eyes —
So close thine,
Thine, dear, thine!

Birds are sleeping in the nest
On the swaying bough,
Thus, against the mother's breast—
So sleep thou—
Sleep, sleep, thou!

Thomas Bailey Aldrich

POEMS: INDEX OF FIRST LINES